Pagan Portals
God-Speaking

Pagan Portals
God-Speaking

Judith O'Grady

Winchester, UK
Washington, USA

First published by Moon Books, 2013
Moon Books is an imprint of John Hunt Publishing Ltd., Laurel House, Station Approach,
Alresford, Hants, SO24 9JH, UK
office1@jhpbooks.net
www.johnhuntpublishing.com
www.moon-books.net

For distributor details and how to order please visit the 'Ordering' section on our website.

Text copyright: Judith O'Grady 2012

ISBN: 978 1 78099 281 5

A CIP catalogue record for this book is available from the British Library.

Design: Stuart Davies

Printed and bound by CPI Group (UK) Ltd, Croydon, CR0 4YY

We operate a distinctive and ethical publishing philosophy in all
areas of our business, from our global network of authors to
production and worldwide distribution.

CONTENTS

Hertha

By Algernon Charles Swinburne

I am that which began;
Out of me the years roll;
Out of me God and man;
I am equal and whole;
God changes, and man, and the form of them bodily; I am the
*   soul.*

Before ever land was,
Before ever the sea,
Or soft hair of the grass,
Or fair limbs of the tree,
Or the fresh-coloured fruit of my branches, I was, and thy soul
*   was in me.*

First life on my sources
First drifted and swam;
Out of me are the forces
That save it or damn;
Out of me man and woman, and wild-beast and bird; before God
*   was, I am...*

Abridged
These are just the opening stanzas,
look up the complete poem for greater enjoyment.

Part 1

Why me? A history of God-Bothered People

I see visions and hear voices. But this book is not about the pharmacopeia or psychoanalysis of treatment but instead about belief; the belief in the Gods that I believe are speaking to me, the belief that They can and do speak to me, and the belief that our communication has some purpose. All of us learn in school that the objects (including ourselves) we see as solid are in fact made up of whirling molecules and are largely emptiness but no one actually falls through their chair when they learn this because we continue to believe that the chair is a solid. Or, to put it a different way, science teachers are dreadfully unconvincing priests. Sometimes when I am arguing with science-believers they categorize my peculiar beliefs as being 'merely perceptual'.

What they mean by this is that my beliefs are 'not real' since the perception and thus the belief is inside my head and not out there in that world made up of loosely connected molecules. But, if you stop to consider it a moment, there is nothing that is not 'merely perceptual' if we are aware of it at all, since none of us are falling through our chairs. Quite a bit has been written about the differences between what we perceive and what the world might be, from the ridiculous ("If a tree falls in the forest and no one is there to hear it does it make a sound?") to the difficult philosophy of Wittgenstein (causing my philosophy professor to leap about on the podium yelling "This!!" "That!!!") but the baseline truth is that each of us perceives from inside our brains, through our faulty senses, and with our preconceptions in place. When any of us agrees with another it is not really 'the Truth' or 'reality' but merely our agreement with each other, 'consensus reality'— that is, what we together have agreed to perceive. There certainly seems to be some outside-of-us realness that we all share; we all need to eat and sleep. Although we vary on what food is; there are cultures that perceive slugs as yummy and others that will find them disgusting unless drenched in garlic butter and named in French (escargot). And when it is appropriate to sleep; siesta or sleeping on the job? But trying to define absolute outside reality is like discussing human instinctual behavior; there is a lot of perceptual reality included and a very scanty amount of unequivocal findings.

The historical way of describing my perceptual reality is to call me a visionary, a seer, or a mystic. All serious words and good ones, but the way I think of it is as a conversational two-way street; I speak to the Gods and They speak to me (if They choose), a process I call 'God-Speaking'. Although the process is less like a telephone conversation and more like a series of prickly feelings and insistent near-insights that ends with conviction rather than understanding. This whole process I call 'God-Bothered' because, really, the Gods don't enter into communication with us to pat us on the back or congratulate us on a job well done but instead to give us difficult tasks and teach us unpleasant truths. It is somewhat of a process to make oneself receptive to speaking with the Gods; there needs to be a natural talent or predilection to begin with that must be nurtured, fostered, trained by meditative trance or, in some cultures, painful ordeal. I also make the assumption that there is some effort required on the part of the Gods to participate in the conversation that only a few of Them are willing to undertake, and that there are a vast number who choose not to trouble Themselves.

All of the societies that I am familiar with (which is lots, but I never feel comfortable making the pronouncement 'all societies') have a place for the person who troubles hirself to speak with the Gods and whom the Gods trouble in return. There is always some trouble in the equation. On the human side, the Gods-Speaker needs to facilitate hir abilities and, it seems, to convince the Gods through some effort that ze is amenable and dedicated. Often and often, the effort is extreme and difficult. As I mentioned, some societies have specific painful ordeal for the apprentice to undertake to show willing. Others leave the inception of the ordeal to the Gods, and identify sickness or trauma given to the chosen one as the initiation ordeal. What process the God undergoes who decides to enter into communication is known only to the Gods. Perhaps They, like many human societies, segregate the Bothering Gods somewhat away from general society. Human societies generally have a way, a place, a tradition, that visionary people can isolate themselves into or be isolated from the usual bustle. As well as the detached dwelling of the Shaman, Medicine Man, or Wise-Woman who lives slightly segregated from the village or the completely separate hut of the hermit there is also the monastery— Buddhist, Hindu, Anglican, or Catholic— all of which allow the God-Bothered people some space to live in that the rest of the community does not enter, both bodily and mentally. Across societies, visionary people generally want to segregate themselves; partly, I find, because the mundane world can be a little intrusive but also because many people find me and other seers a little strange and difficult. Our perceptions are not those of 'normal' people and what we do is troublesome and sometimes dangerous. Indeed, if the society supports the role of shaman/seer/visionary often the other members of the society agree that what the seer is doing can be risky and do not wish to be in too close contact with the process themselves.

This points up the problem of the conflict of duality. A four-way problem, actually— general society has the choice to culturally support or to repudiate the seer and the seer has to choose between seeing hir aptitude as real or delusional. In most 'primitive' societies, there is a clear and society-supported place for the shaman. If you as a people live close to the edge of subsistence, then it makes perfect sense to culturally support the person who negotiates with Greater Spirits for a good outcome for your harvest, hunt, gathering trip, disease, season. As well, it is important to know as soon as possible if the Spirits want something or have an opinion about what the tribe is doing or is contemplating doing and so the person who has good lines of communication with Spirit is important and necessary. In more complex but still faith-based societies (medieval and Northern Europe are what I am most familiar with) the church, while also jumping on any hint of heresy and indulging in a lot of politics, supported visionaries and anchorites and their unique and very person-alized communications with God. It seems that locally a community would support, if not endorse, almost any harmless crazy-thinker as a God-touched hermit much as local communities also supported disabled or differently gifted people. When a God-Bothered Thinker attracted a significant following or preached against received doctrine, the Pope would inevitably get involved— sometimes with a good outcome (Saint Francis of Assisi) and sometimes with a bad (Pelagius). Even ordinary (non-clerical) people, even people who look to our modern eye as incorporating self-aggran-dizing flouncing and self-serving tourism into their trances and visions (Margery Kempe) were generally given the benefit of the doubt by their contemporaries.

Gradually with the onset of the Industrial Revolution, the forming of the Modern and Post-Modern World, and the Deification of Science the World of Faith in which all of the 'primitive' and Pre-Modern peoples lived has faded away. Modern people love to find 'scientific' reasons for actions that were previously faith-based. As an example, people explain Jewish Kosher Laws thusly, 'In old days plates were quite porous and putting meat and dairy on the same imperfectly washed plate resulted in cross-contamination; as people gradually noticed this in a trial-and-error way, a Law was made to accommodate their findings'. But an equally cogent argument can be made that G-d decreed Kosher Laws in order to avoid cross-contamination without explaining to His chosen people the reasoning behind His fiat. The only difference between these two explanations is faith, belief in the presence of G-d and that He cares about and can communicate with His people. Another example, taken from my experience, is that science-based people often use the theory of evolution as an impediment to my belief in a Loving Earth Goddess even in the face of my assertion that Earth made us by means of evolution. I have no problem being both a visionary and a biologist. Not too long ago I was at a Pagan Brunch (a restaurant and a day is chosen and anyone who cares to, comes) and was sitting next to someone (not previously known to me) who categorically stated that "Science replaces Superstition", by which she meant that faith was superseded. When I argued back that 'science' was actually just a means of ascertaining causality by using repeatable experimentation and therefore merely replaced a-causal thinking rather than faith, she was bewildered. I explained further that my experimental world-view was 'the Gods exist' and hers was 'the gods do not exist' but in both cases scientific method could still apply. Finally, she stated that we could "agree to disagree" which translates in Pagan circles into 'I think you are so bat-shit crazy that I no longer wish to discuss the subject with you'.

And that is the crux of the problem for a modern God-Speaker. Being crazy. Actually, being thought to be crazy and being crazy for real, which can be two quite different things.

The less homogenous our societies become, the more wavering and variable the line between charmingly eccentric and dangerously crazy becomes. Modern cultural diversity and the modern ability to know a little about many more of the world's societies than was previously possible, while a good in allowing self-expression, also allows each person to set hir own benchmark of what is real and what is make-believe. People being what they are, this inevitably leads to people either unthinkingly or with prejudice applying their own laws to other peoples' beliefs and opinions. We all like to assume that our thoughts are inescapably right and true and that all we have to do is fully explain them in order to convince the people who disagree with us of their error. This leads to less-than-fun arguments and bafflement. As in the previous example, the non-believer states that anyone using the scientific method must not believe in any Gods rather than that she, as a scientist, does not believe in God. So when I counter that I, a biologist, am an Animist I have stepped not into the realm of differing opinion but into the more difficult place of frankly impossible (to her) and we really have difficulty having a conversation at all. Since I am the minority thinker (even at Pagan Brunch the majority of attendees do not hold the profoundly archaic beliefs that I do) I don't have as much trouble with disagreement as she does; I acknowledge that most people don't have as immense and immediate perception of the Gods as I, I'm a little sorry that they lack what is a meaningful part of belief to me, I carry on trying to convince them— not that they should have such belief, I don't think belief can be mandated— but that starting from my point-of-belief my conclusions are logically consistent.

'Logically consistent' is one of the benchmarks I employ in determining which side of the visionary/crazy line I am on. And, unlike Post-Moderns, I am continually making that distinction. There is a psychological term, 'magical thinking', which is defined as attributing causal effects to a-causal actions. That is, if I rap on the door twice after I lock it upon leaving then my home will not be broken into while I am gone (to make up an example). Or, to use a real example from my beliefs, if I ask for protection and a Dragon curls herself around my yard (in Spirit) to watchfully keep off intruders then my home will not be broken into while I am gone (although I do lock the door because I also believe that the Gods and the Watch-Dragon expect me to behave responsibly). To a Post-Modern, little consideration is required— both of those actions are magical thinking. Since neither one can be shown in repeatable experimentation to keep out intruders they are easily dismissed. For myself and for believers like me, the process is more difficult. Not only do I call up a Dragon, I also use Magical Ward-Runes (made, found, or re-purposed tchotchkes and Magical bric-a-brac) on my doors. I do not believe that the actual salvaged horseshoe is 'Magic' but instead that the presence of the horseshoe reminds me to reference Magic in my daily life and reminds the Gods that I connect to and rely on Their Power. Although I freely admit that if the horseshoe were to come un-nailed and tip out the luck onto the floor I would be concerned. The non-believer makes an easy distinction— all a-causal actions are make-believe. I, on the other hand, believe in both the existence of Magic and the human tendency to attribute causality to unconnected events and so I have to examine each event and make a case-by-case determination of which it is. On the gripping hand, there are people who believe that all events are causal and spend an inordinate amount of time and effort determining every event's causality and insuring that they continue to cause their desired outcome by continuing whatever causal action they have decided on. Those people are crazy. There is a perfectly lovely story I have heard about Carl Jung (the historical famous father of psychoanalysis) and

James Joyce (the historical famous father of the modern novel). Joyce was living in Paris after exiling himself from Ireland and he was brought into contact with Jung by the coterie of intellectuals also residing there. Joyce's daughter was troubled and underwent analysis by Jung, who diagnosed her as schizophrenic. Here the story becomes possibly apocryphal, although still deeply satisfying to me. Joyce did not understand how his daughter could be suffering from a mental illness.

"But the way she thinks is the way I think." he said, "And I am not crazy."

"You are swimming," replied Jung, "She is drowning."

The beauty of this story to me is that there is no absolute distinction between God-Touched (or Muse-Touched) and insane; the distinction lies not in the experience but in the effect of the experience. The crucial question is not 'is this a real experience?' because all experiences are universally distorted to some measure by our perception. The cogent question is 'is this a meaningful and beneficial experience?' I believe that the Gods speak to me, another person believes that I am delusional; we cannot effectively argue our differing beliefs. On the side of the atheist is the lack of quantifiable proof; actions that the unbeliever can use to reliably reproduce my experience. On my side, that of the believer, I have a responsibility to examine the findings that result from my belief. Not to convince the unbeliever (which is demonstrably impossible) but to be confidant that I have received an OtherWorldly message, that I have understood/correctly interpreted it, and that I am willing to do what is requested. The analogy that I use is the difference between quitting smoking and dieting. The unbeliever is like a person quitting smoking— no a-causal events are 'real' and all mind-generated ideas are imaginary— put no more cigarettes into your system. I am like a person deciding to diet— every time

I feel the impulse to eat something I have to consider its caloric weight, its nutritional value, and the sum of what I have already eaten. I may be likely to use some external documentation or resource (a diet plan, a famous nutritionist's book, a dieting group) but ultimately I eat or not (believe or not) of my own will. To extend the analogy, when I receive a message from the Gods I compare it to previous messages for linear comprehension— like a diet plan that makes a categorical statement 'do not eat refined sugar' must then not advise that stirring some jam into your nutritious yoghurt will make it more palatable, if my Gods say 'do not use coercion on adults' (as I believe they do) then They cannot later say that I can use my scary voice to make a dissident stop arguing with me. When I receive a message, I can research in mythos and lore to see if any other God-Bothered people have a similar finding to mine exactly like a dieting person can look up in diet books to see what well-liked food they can safely substitute for an unpalatable one. I can join a worship, research, or discussion group to compare my beliefs and findings with other people's whose opinions I value and to stimulate me in my endeavors just like a dieting person can have a group or buddy to keep them exercising and making good food choices. All of these tools— logic, research, and discussion— are useful and I suggest employing them. There are also some basic rules that I find helpful:

The Gods rarely, if ever, tell us to do what we want to do and were planning to do anyway; the Gods are logically consistent (They do not change Their minds) and do not abrogate our free will (They do not force us to do Their will); the directives of the Gods are often unpleasant and surprising although not outside our capabilities. To refer back to my example of dieting: the Gods are not prompting you to eat birthday cake so as to not offend the birthday person, really tasty jam is still sugar and not irresistible, if it's Canadian winter outside you should join a gym rather than give up jogging. Or to use myself as an example, the Gods do not send me entertaining reading as a means of excusing me from research; the Goddess to Whom I am dedicated keeps asking me to do things that consistently end up with my being engaged in religious writing; and those requests are persistently about group and public interaction which I find shy-making and uncomfortable. Although I can always choose to not do those things and can choose not to write but can instead choose to read dated low-violence mysteries from the second-hand bookstore which were not sent to me by the Gods, it is by doing those things asked of me that I gradually see the meaningfulness and design in the requests and messages. As well, there is the amassment of a personal body of evidence about the messages themselves; the similarity of a new message to other tested and verified messages that gives it additional believability. For example, when I hear/see/think something that is a message it comes with what I describe as 'an ethereal clang'. That is, there is a subliminal sense of the reverberations caused by a much larger space than the inside of my head, a sort of mystical echo. So hearing that causes me to pay more attention to the message received even though I still apply the guidelines of consistency, difficulty, and research to it. I also feel that everyone who is God-Bothered, has meaningful belief, or thinks and formulates ideas should welcome the opportunity for intelligent discussion. The process of explaining and delineating ideas and belief is supremely clarifying; it's like reading poetry aloud— one realizes on the visceral level what doesn't work and needs revision, where one is skimming over the logical process and substituting wishful thinking. Although there are limits and boundaries to be respected— for example I explain to my sister (who is deeply committed to pit-bull rescue) that although I acknowledge abuse I choose not to see photos of abuse victims so she doesn't send me them. In the same vein, I refuse to discuss my beliefs with people whose bottom line is that I am going to the Tedious Lake of Fire, just as I will stop explaining evolutionary theory to a person who counters with the argument, "Mules!". In the end, I ask for and give acceptance but not suspension of disbelief— if someone tells me that the Moon is made of blue cheese and eaten away monthly by the Mouse in the Moon I will immediately ask where the new moon comes from. If the Blue-Cheese Believer has a linear mythos about the Inter-dimensional Dairy Goddess I will stop arguing but not start believing. If someone asks for my help in receiving messages from the Gods I will facilitate but if I receive a message that the person declines to believe I will not try to convince hir. I accept that my World-View is outside 'normal' and I don't ask for endorsement although I relish debate and enjoy agreement.

There is another psychological term, 'disassociation', which means (roughly) 'no longer present and conscious'. 'Trance' or 'Astral Travel', the process by which myself and many others travel to 'away' and receive input from Spirit, is indistinguishable from 'disassociation' to the outside observer. As in the differentiation between magical thinking in psychology and Magical Events in belief, the only real difference is inside the experience. In the perceptions of the trance magician, ze is going somewhere else and interacting with a Spirit Being. In the perceptions of the psychological observer, the subject is no longer aware of outside reality. If you believe in trancing, the seer is Elsewhere talking to the Gods. If you do not, the dissociative individual is locked in hir brain having a delusional experience.

In history and in 'primitive' cultures distinguishing between dangerously or harmfully crazy people and visionary seers is well covered by the societal template. Seers and Shamans are often demanding and difficult people but clearly work for the betterment of the tribe; crazy people are destructive. After extensive thought, I have decided that the baseline commandment of the Gods is that neither They nor we should use coercion— They leave us free will and we should give others the same. A friend of mine formulates the supreme commandment as, "don't be a douche" which I support. Many different believers have a similar stricture, "do unto others as you would have them do unto you" or, in more modern language, "do as you would be done by" or, the more Pagan-ish, "what you do returns to you". So, to clarify with an example, a message from the Gods that I should plant trees is likely valid— it asks me for effort and it betters the living world. A message from the Gods that I should preach tree-planting is still believable although I am being asked for less effort and am influencing if not compelling others. If I hear that the Gods will put any trees planted by my acolytes on my Spirit credit balance without any planting effort on my part I am likely telling myself a story. People who climb up and live in trees to prevent them from being cut down, while far outside society-normal, are dedicating themselves; people who hammer spikes in trees to maim loggers are listening to bad voices.

And I believe that there are bad voices. People can be destructively crazy without reference to the Gods at all and, in a universe filled with innumerable Gods, there are surely Gods who are not very interested in the betterment of Their people as well as those who don't like people at all and those who enjoy causing trouble without reference to the outcome. So the seer needs discernment as well as belief. The metaphor I use is 'riding the Crazy-Train'. I go into trance, and I am offered a vision— I am at the station and the Crazy-Train pulls in. I can choose to embark or to stay where I am. With me on it or not, the Crazy-Train pulls away. I (if I have chosen to) ride along looking at the scenery. Other stations occur, and I can get off at Ask-A-Question Junction or Find-Your-Totem Halt if I decide to. Beings may enter my car or compartment and sit down for a chat, if I respond. I will not descend onto the dark, graffitied, broken-down platform of Destructive Thinking even though it too is a stop on the line. The train will eventually pull into the terminus and I will be able to tour the immense and impressively glittering station of Visionary Experience before I either die (always a slight possibility especially in traditional societies) or travel back where I came from largely unchanged except for new and significant knowledge.

When I am discussing trance with someone to whom it is a new idea, they will generally (very politely since I am a Canadian) raise the possibility that I am delusional.

"Could you not be ... ummmmmmmm ... "

"Crazy?" I respond.

"Welllllll, perhaps wishful thinking ... ?"

Most of the time I find this charming and well-intentioned; the questioner is helpfully trying to prevent my destructive loss of sanity. When I assure them that this is not a new idea to me they are both reassured and horrified; I am not offended and am guarding against insanity but at the same time I am willing to do something that might have an unforeseen and possibly dangerous outcome. Post-Moderns do not like the idea that I will abrogate my own will and do the bidding of an unseen Goddess without knowing what the result will be. Historical and 'primitive' peoples had no such squeamish problems with God-directed activities. As well, not only did their cultures have a recognized place for the God-Bothered seer but the newbie visionary would generally be accepted and mentored by an established shaman. As an apprentice the adjustment, accommodation, and expansion of powers would be both safer and more understandable to 'normal' society. In a Post-Modern First World culture, the newfound seer is either constrained into hiding what is happening and how their perceptions are changing or is immediately marginalized. On the edges of 'normalcy', there are both people and Gods who are interested in acolytes without giving due consideration to causing harm to them or to their wishes. Indeed, there are people and Gods who demand acting against one's self-interest as a proof of love or trust or belief, but you don't have to comply with those requests. The Good Gods are not petty or vengeful, and are likely to offer you some other means of expression if Their first offer is too difficult. Remember that there is a great big station of Outright Crazy on the train line— don't get off there and don't drink the cool-aid from the vendor there.

Part 2

Why Pagan? History and NeoPagans

So if any God can visit our minds or join us on the Crazy-Train what directs me to choose to be a Pagan, a Many-Gods believer, and an Animist, a Spirit-in-Everything believer, and therefore marginalize myself not only from non-seers but also from mainstream religion? Because although belief in the Gods is a choice— I have free will and can choose to not believe just as I can choose to not act— I am constrained by the choice that the Gods make as well. I was in a discussion with a devout Jesus-Believer who (to her honor and discernment) could clearly perceive that I am a genuinely religious person. She asked why I had not asked Jesus into my heart (but in a pleasant, fact-finding way rather than in a proselytizing way, thus ensuring that I would continue to discuss the question with her). I explained to her that I didn't make a requisition but an offer; I opened up my heart and Jesus was not Who arrived. Of course her next thought was that I, if not delusional, was being tricked and deluded by what she, with the One-God rule, defined as a 'demon'. My answer to that is that if I invite/open my heart exclusively to the Good Gods then only the Good Gods are able to answer. I believe that the Good Gods are more powerful than the Bad Ones because creation and creativity are Their purview. The Bad Gods are in charge of deception, destruction, and plagiarism, and in order to communicate exclusively with Them (or to listen to demons as a Christian) one has to relentlessly exclude the promptings of one's conscience and ignore the messages of positivism. Of course, not all believers agree that the Good Gods are stronger than the Evil Ones. And some people, Christian and Pagan both, prefer to ignore the possibility of directed and implemented Evil as a force outside people's minds or as separate from omission (the absence of Good) rather than as commission (performing bad acts). Everyone has to decide what they believe for themselves, although I see plenty of evidence for personified Evil myself. Apart from the absolute of Who answers when I invite interaction there is also a personal bias I have towards Paganism as being often defined as a 'Nature Religion' and thus very attractive to a biologist. 'Nature', which I define as 'the squishy, complex, and fascinating systems that make up everything' not only defines my world but also who I am and what I find to be meaningful and so is the obvious religious direction for me. Patriarchal and One-God religious systems are just not very interesting nor compelling to me; in biology nothing is completely in control and there are no immutable laws dispensed by One Being. Also, as a biologist I am predisposed to interacting and mutually beneficial systems as a template— this helps me and you both, your assistance now ensures my survival and assistance later— rather than a dualistic system based on Law— right/wrong, good/bad, true/false. So I choose to be a Pagan. But Pagans as well as more mainstream believers and also outright non-believers bring a modern perspective to their perceptions, separating Nature from their everyday lives. I find the post-modern disenfranchisement from Nature as ridiculous— the force that cracks the sidewalk and the weed that grows up from it are 'Nature' as much as the primordial forest. When we splash death-dealing pesticides and balance-tottering fertilizers on the Earth we didn't get those ingredients from Outer Space; it is our use of them rather than their origin that is unnatural. Most of the Pagans I converse with are First-World, city-dwelling, well-educated, middle class people who tend to see themselves as the center the world revolves around. They see themselves as powerful— do they not control their environments both winter and summer, can they not eat out-of-season or pre-processed foods at whim, are they not able to vacation wherever in the world they wish and have fruity drinks on demand— and as special— are they not managers and team-leaders, do they not have unique abilities, education, and powers, can they not afford the latest in technology and use the freshest and most incomprehensible jargon? Not only do they see themselves as having free will but as having a larger-than-life will— 'if I will it I can change reality'. If reality fails to be changed at their command they do not then acknowledge that reality is the larger and more powerful but that they experienced a failure of will which practice will make perfect. So they tend to approach interactions with the Gods as being something like 'taking a meeting'; they will pencil it in on their schedule and the Gods will reciprocate. In the modern spirit of immediate gratification modern Pagans are often unwilling to put in lengthy unrewarded effort before they see any result. In my life I have very little trouble with these things; I grow a perennial garden and I have been planting trees for thirty years. Perennials only start to come into their own several years after they are planted and often the garden is not much like what was envisioned by that time apart from the longest-lasting hardscape. The trees I planted thirty years ago are barely full grown and live in other yards than my current one. I am not the powerful and special being in this transaction, the trees and plants are. Empowerment is a very post-modern concept in the way it is currently defined as empowering any member of a minority, disenfranchised or marginalized person, or 'differently abled' individual to demand special treatment in order to level their benefits or equalize their treatment into balance with the perceived benefits and treatment of the majority.

Historically, though, power is something you take, not

something you legislate or demonstrate for. There is a wonderful concept put forth in the excellent book *Cattle Lords And Clansmen* by Nerys Patterson:

A powerful clan leader can own more cows (cows are wealth) than he actually has the grass for by loaning cows to his clients. They keep them, retain the offspring, and give their lord a set number of dinners a year. When the Old Lord dies a New Lord is chosen and one of the pivotal demonstrations of the New Lord's fitness is that the clients acknowledge his continued ownership of the Old Lord's loaned-out cows. If he doesn't have the power to enforce this, no amount of whining about fairness or the decision of the derbfine (the lord-selecting body) as binding could bring the rowdy clients into control. So for me the post-modern spectacle of demonstration is backwards. Demanding that the people in power (the clients who are holding your cows) acknowledge your ownership because of 'fairness' or 'justice' is ineffective. Taking away the client's or government's power (cattle-raiding or choosing to buy a different product, support a different legislator, or enact a different law) is effective. Refusing to comply is something anyone can do if they choose to while making someone else, particularly someone in a position of power, comply with your wishes is much more problematical. This concept, that the voice of the people conveys power, seems to be modern (linked to democracy) but is ancient. Any leader, no matter how despotic or imbued with Divine Right, can find hirself without followers, un-listened to and un-attended. This demonstration of complete emptiness— 'no one is listening to you' —is more congruent with my ideals and is more historically apt (and also an Irishism— look up Captain Charles Boycott). The perception of your personal power as well as the belief that Powers have been given to you by the action of the Gods is not justified by the depth of belief on the part of the seer but the outcome of the interactions between oneself and the Gods and the interactions between the seer and their culture. The idea that empowerment is a marginalized person's right seems to me likely to be unenforceable although I wouldn't ever stop anyone from trying. However, the completely modern idea that all people are equal is, for me, the turning point upon which the shift from Then to Now rests.

Equality is a peculiarly modern concept. While I am at best ambivalent about 'empowerment' I wholly endorse equality. Many years ago I was co-opted into an historical re-enactment group and kitted up as a settler at the time of the American Revolution. I was a little grudging about it; I am just not good at pretending and I would absolutely refuse to not wear sun-blocking corrective-lens glasses so as to give myself an historical headache and trip over things. Once, my sponsoring 'Lady' (an enthusiastic pretender) went to the Commander of the Army (and a flash lot of gear he wore, himself) to request something and, after being granted an audience and before speaking, curtseyed to him. I, hanging in the background, was appalled. In the same vein when I began my Pagan-Path journey as a youngster I found myself barred by personal stubbornness from choosing Wicca because coveners address their coven leaders as 'my lord' and 'my lady'. I deny the addition of fancy trousers and a sword as necessitating a curtsey, and I bend the knee and use respectful address to the Gods, not other people. I do not perceive people as interchangeably equal pegs but as distinguished by their actions and beliefs rather than by their born-in-life station or the number of cows they claim.

On the one hand, there have always been common people. In the same narrow-focus way that modern people view untouched ecologies and only them as 'Nature' modern people also tend to lump themselves into what they perceive as an attractive historically empowered group. 'Druids were the lawyers and professors of the past; I am a Modern Druid', 'The Warrior Class were paramount; I am a Modern Warrior', 'Clan Leaders were absolute rulers; I am a Modern Clan-Lord'. All that I know of my ancestors show them to have been fisher-folk and farmers; I am the undoubted descendant of peasants and myself a Modern Small-Holder. No castles then nor now. In a close study of folklore, however, peasants are shown to have a meaningful belief system and fulfilling lives almost wholly unconnected to the greater folk's battles and enchantments that roiled around them. That study is what I find interesting, meaningful, and admirable and the source of the life style I aim to model. Not the professorial 'Druid Religious Leader' but the rural-dwelling, canny, Cunning-Woman or Wort Doctor (like Biddy Early) is who I am trying to emulate.

On the other hand, history always has to be read and understood in the context of history. We cannot deny that people in history were often egregiously defunct in modern values. Take slavery as an obvious and terrible example. Because Thomas Jefferson not only owned slaves but had slave descendants does that negate his contributions to the historical perception of freedom? No, it is disheartening that he failed in personal perception but what he said, did, and wrote can still be true and valuable. Enlarging that idea, the perception of 'slavery' as being embodied by Africans being kidnapped and exploited by immigrant Europeans as a New-World labour force is also narrow and modern — all pre-industrial agricultural cultures (that I am aware of) employed slaves. Often those owned people had the same skin color and background as their owners and had to be depersonalized and enslaved by quite small differences; they were from a non-dominant religion, had poor family or were poor themselves, did not own land, had committed crimes or had family members who committed crimes, had been on the losing side in armed conflict, etc. What allows us as modern people to express the idea that slavery is 'wrong'? Our resounding and impeccable morals or the advent of mechanical labor-saving devices? Still, to be able to perceive that all people have an inalienable right to not be property is a good, even if something other than perfect ideals allow the perception to be accepted and flourish. And while we cannot endorse the owning of people today because our ancestors (everybody's ancestors, bar none) owned people we can also acknowledge that the act of historical ownership of slaves does not vilify any other praiseworthy thing our ancestors or historical role-models might have done. Gradually, with many slippages of perception skewing 'goodness' as an attribute of 'richness' or 'attractiveness' or 'powerfulness' we are formulating a system of meritocracy, where the actions of the person demonstrate their value. The concept of 'God-selected King' or 'well-born nobility' fades into the past.

On the gripping hand, what does the now-outdated class system show us? That once there were people with special attributes (kingly, noble, high-born) who had special responsibilities. Brehon Law, the Ancient Irish legal system, and the Irish king-making mythos clearly exemplify this. Just as in the example of the clan-leader and the cows, power rested in how many people looked to you for leadership rather than in how many people were constrained to owe you fealty as in the Norman system. If you were only responsible for yourself you were a poor weak being, but if you were responsible for a whole family/tribe/kingdom of people (and they agreed with your 'rule') then you were powerful. But then you were also responsible for the well-being of your people in an immediate and connected way. If they suffered, whether from disease or catastrophe, it was their lord's responsibility to see them put right. One paradigm for this is the story of the Three Little Pigs: the Wolf (hard times) comes to the door of your straw-built house and destroys it and you. You run to your neighbor's house of sticks (these are the old kind of commonfolk's dwelling, wattle-and-daub) but hard times subsume him as well. Both of you run to the Lord, who lives in a house of stone. He shelters you and defeats the Boogey-Wolf. In the Irish Mythos, if he was unable to kill the Wolf the act of his being defeated would be an indication of his unfitness as lord. Another example is in the ancient story of Nuada as told in the *First Battle of Mag Tuired (Cét-chath Maige Tuired)* where the High King loses his arm in battle. He is then unable to remain king because the king must be physically perfect, and the story goes on to debate whether his replacement silver arm is sufficient with a side-jaunt into physician (and father and son) jealousy and contention. As a modern person, I always had trouble with this story— why does losing his arm unfit him for kingship? Particularly when he has a prosthesis, what is essentially different or changed about him? After years of puzzlement, I realized that I was looking at the story backwards. In the modern ethos, handicapped does not equate with incapable and there are many people perfectly willing to back that assumption up with laws and strong feelings. In the Ancient Irish world-view, the fact that the King lost an arm indicated that he had previously become incapable and losing an arm was merely the physical demonstration of his failure to qualify as kingly. Another example of this belief is mentioned in the sequel to Nuada's story, the *Last Battle of Mag Tuired (Cath Dédenach Maige Tuired)*. The land bears poorly and the people suffer famine because their King, Bres, is inhospitable. So what happens to the leader of the people is in part a reflection of the state of well-being in the land ze is a ruler of and the actions of the leader reflect onto the land ze is leading directly, causing good general outcome from specific good actions and vice versa.

This is what I, as an archaic thinker, define as 'Sovereignty';

the recognition of the ruler by the Gods and the acceptance of the ruler by the people. The derbfine (three generations of people connected by kinship to the previous King) selects the new ruler. First, the people ruled exercise their power to agree or disagree by following the chosen leader or by supporting some other champion. Then, the Gods show Their approval or disapproval by what happens— war or peace, good harvests or famine, well-being or pestilence. In response to what happens (if they are paying attention or correctly interpret events) the people continue or withdraw their support. So the Gods or some of the Gods (perhaps the Local Gods are more interested in the selection of Kings) are in communication with the rulers and, indirectly, with the ruled tribespeople as well as with the specifically chosen and trained God-Speakers of the tribe. The King, in making the Great Marriage with the Land (in the societies I am familiar with this is a very specific and elaborate ceremony replete with opportunities for communication and omens), agrees to listen to the opinion of the Gods about how well the reign is going and what needs to be done to enhance it. The Gods agree that They acknowledge the King's fitness and will send omens and communications to the ruler, to the ruler's advisors and God-bothered seers, and to the people living on the land being ruled. Although this in history presupposes a class system, in its workings-out it becomes a meritocracy. Even if the chosen King is correctly born (as Bres was in the old lore of Ireland) if he behaves badly then he will be supplanted (in this case eventually by Lugh who is no better born but a better, more skilled, and nobly behaved champion).

How does Sovereignty translate into the Post-Modern World? On the one hand, we could pass legislation that pestilence or famine as well as a vote of no confidence would precipitate a national election. On the other hand, we could try to re-establish the class society and the Monarchy. Since few citizens agree with my world-view these decrees would likely be problematical to enforce. On the gripping hand what seems best is to acknowledge what is, and to give each citizen the rights and responsibilities of a ruler as well as a member of their society. In history the Gods involved in Sovereignty spoke only to Kings and God-Speakers but They are now constrained to speak to whomever will talk to Them. Democracy has overthrown Kingship; each person becomes the tiny equivalent of a King and so, in my world-view, has the responsibilities of a ruler.

Part 3A

Belief and Ritual ... Why Gods?

In one of my most favourite Irish stories, Finn MacCool (or Fionn mac Cumhaill) the Giant, Hero, and Leader of the Fianna is relaxing with the warrior band he leads and poses the question, "What is the most beautiful sound in the world?"

The various band members suggest answers— "the clang of sword on shield", "the sigh of a maiden satisfied", "the lullaby a mother sings to her baby" — but Finn rejects them all. Finally he is asked what he deems the most beautiful sound; "The sound of what happens is the most beautiful sound in the world." he answers.

As in all essential Irish stories, the 'moral' is complex and not easily accessible, and can be studied at length in much the same way that Zen koan can be studied. What is Finn MacCool saying? All sounds are patently not equally attractive and sometimes what happens is outright unpleasant. But what happens is the starting point, the necessary going-on-from place, and all action and reaction devolves from it. This is the same concept as the fifth direction, 'where I am', which is added to the four cardinal directions. 'What happens' is in time what 'where you are' is in place and the point of here-and-now.

Rather than begin with a linear mythos, 'When and how were the Gods created?' I use the same experiential format that science uses and the injunction of Finn as my starting point. Rather than first look for a logical, or at least emotionally satisfying and linear, creation story I work to experience what exists outside my normal perception at this moment. Research, both reading and practicing, suggests avenues of approach for stepping outside ordinary experience. Once some visionary experience is achieved, research again can help suggest what similar experiences other seers have had and what meaning they extracted from them. In other words, I learned to trance and while in trance state, I sent out a greeting. Someone answered, and I then had to communicate with Hir about what Ze might want to say while cautiously protecting myself from madness and delusion. Gradually I built up a body of visionary experiences, generally called 'personal gnosis' meaning 'stuff I comprehend from visionary sources' and sometimes dismissed as 'UPG' (unverified personal gnosis) meaning 'stuff that fell into my head without sourcing' by scholars wishing to make a strong sometimes pejorative distinction between gnosis and textual research. I compare my personal gnosis with that of other visionaries and with ancient texts of myths to see what points of correspondence there are.

Not surprisingly, the Irish mythos uses a Finn MacCool-like format; there is no actual Irish creation myth. On the one hand, this is a sad lack. There is no charming, world-licking cow, Auðhumla, as in the Norse. On the other hand, perhaps there was a creation myth that was not written down by the myth-preserving monks or saved by canny Irish storytellers but if so then we can never know what it was. On the gripping hand, there is the *Book of Invasions (Lebor Gabála Érenn)* which tells what happened. On one level, what the Book tells the scholar is very simple, 'We came to Ireland from elsewhere. These are the Gods Who travelled with us. These are the Gods we found there when we came. This is the resolution we achieved.' It is a story about 'what is', not a story about 'how this came to be' or 'what was at the beginning'.

So, when I trance away and speak with Someone, where did that Being come from? Elsewhere. It is apparent that even while I am not in my customary space neither is Whomever I am speaking with. If, as I explained before, I am riding the Crazy-Train into trance then both of us are on the trip and have met at some intermediary station to converse. Just as I have chosen to leave human-space, the God has chosen to leave Gods-Space. I assume that the God makes this choice with a better comprehension of what Ze is going to find, with whom Ze is going to meet, and what motivations Ze has for traveling off to interact with me than I do. I define myself as an 'archaic thinker', that is I hold beliefs and ideals that are quite distanced from the average post-modern believer. One of these 'old' beliefs is that the Gods are big. Timeless, wise, philosophical, powerful; and motivated by a greater under-standing and comprehension than I have access to. I have had many arguments about the nature of the Gods with dedicated followers of many Pagan Paths who persistently describe the Gods as "friends", "allies", and "partners" that they "work with", form maternal or paternal or sisterly or brotherly bonds with, or enter into equal and sexual relationships with. This seems to me like a terrible waste of time— why trance elsewhere in order to communicate with someone much like oneself?

The Gods who communicate with me come from Gods-Land and are definitively more in charge of the conversation than I am. So I do not get to quiz Them on what Gods-Land looks like, what Their creation mythos is, and what Their exact relationship with each other is. Sometimes nuggets of fact will come up, as in "this part of your concern is not part of My domain" or "your reasoning is flawed, the end result will be different than you expect" but the Gods do not explain Their workings to me nor do I expect Them to. That being said, because They are using my perceptions to communicate with the communications necessarily come in a format that I can comprehend. I am only fluent in English and so the Gods speak to me in English. My presumption is that They are speaking Godish and I am hearing English and that another person would hear the message in their language of choice. An argument can be made that if one wants to communicate with the 'Old' Gods that it is necessary to learn the language in which the God one wants to communicate with was addressed by in history, and it is a good argument. It is polite to show the Gods effort and dedication when addressing Them and learning an old and now little-used language is difficult and time consuming. As well, the Gods who choose to communicate only in that language will never talk to a modern-language speaker no matter what lengths they might go to. However if those Gods are not speaking to me I have no way of knowing it and must rely on the communications that come to me in English. Similarly, I am familiar with the myths and stories of Ireland (in translation) and so They will use examples from, often have the appearance of, and reference the culture I am familiar with. What do They look like when They're at home? Not apprehensible to me.

Many post-modern Pagans, latching on to the undoubted fact that belief is inside the believer's mind rather than a part of external reality, believe that we create the Gods ourselves by our power of mind. Some believe that we create the Gods wholly, and some that we perceive aspect or facets of the One God-Being as individuals because of our various cultures or personal idiosyncrasies. People being both similar and different at all times, sometimes one person's or culture's perception of possibly related Gods is remarkably similar to another's and sometimes the perception of the same God is remarkably inconsistent. There are two opposing human impulses at work; one is conflation and the other is not. Conflation is nothing new, the Romans became masters of it as they tramped across Europe, 'We have a God who is connected to thunder, you have a God also connected to thunder ... your God is our God by a different Name'. New

Age Post-Moderns do the very same thing, 'Look at all the cultures that have a Kindly Mother Goddess ... Kindly Mother Goddess has a multitude of Names'. Equally strong but oppositional is the human desire for specialness and rightness. 'My Love Goddess rides around in a chariot pulled by cats and has nothing to do with sea foam, your Love Goddess is nothing like.'

Added to this is the human habit of making things make sense and be orderly and linear. Many cultures over-run by the Romans liked the new Gods or the new definitions of their Gods the Romans brought and happily added new names, attributes, and stories to the extant ones or adjusted the extant stories to reflect the new suppositions. When cultures came into contact (or when we as moderns study the mythos and stories of different ancient cultures), often there were new and attractive ideas, Gods, and beliefs that one culture would adopt from another. Modern Pagans agonize over this or agonize over other Pagans doing this or, sometimes, agonize over this not being done enough. In general, Neo-Pagan thought embraces syncretism, defined by the Oxford Dictionary as "the amalgamation or attempted amalgamation of different religions, cultures, or schools of thought" and generally used to mean 'what my beliefs embody' and looks down on eclecticism, defined by that dictionary as "deriving ideas, style, or taste from a broad and diverse range of sources" and generally used as 'what people with whom I disagree believe'. However, even the strictest of Reconstructionism Pagans has to admit that cultures which were once very close diverged over time and space to be similar but not exactly the same. On the other end of the spectrum there are frank Eclectic Pagans who merely use whatever forms they find attractive.

What becomes clear in examining Pagan beliefs is that the Gods are like subatomic particles. If I understand physics and quantum field theory (which of course I do not) then the study of subatomic particles changes their nature, leaving us to formulate theories about what we have perceived and make assumptions about what might have been there before we perceived it. In the question of our perception of the Gods, clearly our perception can never completely apprehend the nature of the Gods and we have little or no outside evidence to work with. Useless to dig a big hole miles across in order to track a God whizzing by to be measured.

The Gods at home in Gods-Land are not subject to our scrutiny at all; we do not see Them until They have manifested in our minds and are therefore colored by our perceptions. However, there is a group of Gods that have an external focus; one that is outside our individual mind. These are the Gods of Place, who have been commented on in all places and all times. Rivers, hills, volcanoes, forests, and wells all have indwelling Spirits; and in modern times cities and constructed place-markers are also seen to be inhabited. This practice and belief raises an interesting question— how does an indwelling Spirit get there? Undeniably, the interest given to Indwelling Spirits by humans has some effect; as in physics, interaction changes the nature of the thing studied. Some Pagans firmly believe that the energy put into a place by humans creates the Spirit. To me this is ludicrously anthropocentric. Anthropocentric is defined by the Oxford Dictionary as "regarding humankind as the central or most important element of existence, especially as opposed to God or animals" and a wonderful word to use when debating with post-modern Neo-Pagans; very few people will admit that you have just used a word they don't know the meaning of and so my statement becomes very hard for them to disagree with. In my archaic thinking, the Spirits of Place are still bigger than I am. They must, I believe, have seen a space being made by human intention and energy, or noticed a beautiful or meaningful space in the natural world and decided to visit from Gods-Land and stay there, adding some aspect of that place to their seeming appearance to humans when They communicate with them.

So, if we avoid small-minded human thinking and look at this question from a larger perspective, the in-dwelling Spirit does not come at the behest or exhortation of the human nor does the human create the Spirit. The Spirit must have some reason sufficient to Hirself for entering into a place; Ze must 'want' to. The In-dwelling Spirit must get some benefit from bringing at least some part of Hirself from Gods-Land and confining that part of Hirself to one place. Some part of it must be the attributes of the place chosen— the sound of running water, the strength of great trees, the special taste of the well-water, the view from the mountain. Some part must be the company of sympathetic and like-minded beings— the trees in the forest, the animals the place shelters, the similar Indwelling-Spirits sharing Their experiences on some Gods-Plane, and the people who love, appreciate, and communicate with the Spirit of the Place. Also, the most meaningful of all, the communion with the Goddess of the Complete Place, the Mother Earth. As a biologist, I am very aware of how systems which seem to be one being are actually a lot of beings clubbing together (like sponges) and beings that seem to be a lot of unconnected beings are actually one system (like termites). Humans like to think of themselves as a single being, but that is not only anthropocentric but also just plain wrong. We could not digest food without our gut bacteria, for example, but we prefer not to think of ourselves merely as a life-support system for their comfort. Even more telling, no living beings at all would exist without mitochondria (google it up, they are way cool). Mitochondria live as individual beings in all of our cells and we, comprised of these many beings, consider ourselves as a single living being and self-aware. Obviously, we are imperfectly self-aware since we can communicate with neither our gut bacteria nor our mitochondria. But this concept forms a template that we can apply in a different way. What if we are the mitochondria and the Earth Herself is the Living Being that is also a system? She, unlike ourselves and our bacteria, parasites, and organelles, is truly Self-aware and can communicate with her many parts, as well as those Spirits of Place or Events who have come to live here on the Earth.

This is a recognized biological theory, the Gaia hypothesis, named after the Greek Goddess. Biology shies away from identifying a Being as a Goddess even when using divine names, but the theory inescapably defines the Earth Organism as powerful and directed. As a believer as well as a biologist, I add wise as an attribute. I am not much moved by nor knowledgeable about the Greek Pantheon; I incline to the more Northern Name of Hertha (influenced by a deep appreciation of the Swinburne poem) but also commonly use the Name Earth or Mother Earth, a Goddess-Name that everyone recognizes. If we look at what Earth has done in Her physical manifestation and try to draw conclusions about Her intentions, it seems that She has acted to create life on Herself. By actions too numerous to discuss at length: the properties of water, the amount and salinity of the oceans, the action of amino acid chains, global forestation and plankton, the interaction between carbon dioxide and oxygen— She has fostered the occurrence of life. Clearly, She feels quite differently about being covered with living things than we feel about our eyelash mites. I think that She loves life.

But life in general is one thing and human beings are a much different set of beings. Humans are a peculiar end-point in the process of evolution. Much discussion has been bruited about trying to define the difference between humans and other animals. Even without bringing in the, in my opinion, outdated Abrahamic Biblical concept of special creation and our contract with Jehovah for dominance there are differences between ourselves and our genetically almost indistinguishable cousins the chimpanzees. We use tools. Well, not only chimps but even some birds have been seen to use tools. We speak. Well, that is due in part to the construction of our throats and indeed there are a few primates that have learned to sign as well as the possibly conversing parrot. Some of us are sometimes altruistic ... that's just feeble. We keep written records and transmit cultural ideals and we, up until recently when a few post-moderns felt themselves to be above it, worshipped. If you accept the Gaia Hypothesis, then this must be a desirable end-point. Are we then the culmination of evolution? The perfect zenith of Life? The tiny, sharp point of the pyramid of all living beings?

To me this is ludicrously anthropocentric. Just as, in the beginning of the chapter, Finn did not specify a specific part or kind of "what happens" but accepted all of it, Earth deals with what grows. All reality is by mutual consensus and evolution is a random process. Earth nurtures life, allows life to be and develop. By a series of accidental mutations and naturally selected but haphazard events we are what happens. Language-using and specifically the ability to speak to and be spoken to by the Gods seems to have been manipulated into the brains of a promising line of proto-simians but having longer hair-coat on our heads, as one example, is likely accidental. Earth has gone to a lot of trouble to have God-Speakers about, and the Gods actively foster the skill when we develop it and respond when we use it. They are lonely by Themselves and want to chat.

Part 3B

Belief and Ritual ... Why Worship?

A natural extension of the theory that Mother Earth is sentient and has had an important part in our creation is the supposition that She has used evolution to help bring this about. I, along with many others, hold this belief. But we also have mysterious and apparently useless attributes that are not brought about by a logical application of natural selection. Love of beauty, for example, does not seem to be selected for:

"Look at the beautiful sunset!" says Caveperson 1

Caveperson 2 looks around distractedly, not interested in pink clouds ... "Eeek! A tiger!" and runs away.

"Yum!" says Tiger, munching up Caveperson 1

And yet love of beauty is universal; 'primitive' people spend hours adorning themselves, decorating their pots and baskets, making jewelry, and frescoing their walls and using up time that could be more logically spent grubbing up roots or domesticating load-bearing animals. What is beautiful is culturally and personally determined, one person's treasure is always another's trash, but the good feeling that possessing and even just viewing beautiful things causes in the viewer is a universal; a desirable feeling that they will spend their funds on or travel to the museum or opera-house to experience. More importantly the creation of beauty, the creative process, is intensely felt by the artist. Even when the creative process is being experienced by an artist who uses words it is so miraculous, so ineffably wonderful, as to be a nonverbal feeling that remains largely inexpressible. However, artists of all kinds try to express what they feel when in the grip of the creative moment and agree with each other about many of the aspects of that experience. Artists

35

often use 'the feeling of rightness' or 'being in the groove' or 'swept away' to define the process of making artistically satisfying creations or choosing the next steps in the process of creation. As well, they often include the awareness of an outer source of direction in the description; 'the words were put into my head', 'my hand was guided', 'the concept came to me'.

Although how brains work is by no means clearly understood, we have been able to see by means of electrodes and newer imaging technology what part of the brain is being used during different mental exercises. Remembering uses a different part of the brain than theorizing, for example. Being enrapt in the creative process uses a part of the brain that is also used in meditation. There is a tiny part of the brain that 'lights up' (transfers an electrical signal) quite strongly when the person has what they describe as a mystical experience. Communicating with or being communicated to by the Gods uses a specific part of the brain no matter how the individual personifies, conceives, or believes. I refer to this part of the brain as the 'Gods-Speaker'. Since this is a one-use bit of brain there is absolutely no naturally selected reason for it to be there unless Gods-Speaking has a purpose. The way I see it, Earth wants the beings who seem to be evolving to fill the niche of self-aware communicating beings to be able to speak with the Gods and to receive messages from Them and so She inserts the Gods-Speaker into our developing brains (back when we're poking each other with sharp sticks) so that we will have this capacity. Then when we evolve to the point of 'culture' and are interested in being spoken to by Earth and the other Gods we have the necessary receptor already imbedded and can hear the advice and requests They wish to communicate to us.

The belief that Earth put the Gods-Speaker in our developing brains is, while not unique to me, an unusual belief. The belief that one's God/dess/s/desses (whatever number and gender or universality and lack of gender one's belief encompasses) can and do communicate with at least some of Their believers is almost universal. Even post-modern religious thought in which there is no longer a place nor training for the God-Bothered person still allows for the believer to designate messages as being 'from God', although those people will be likely to also undergo psychological examination and decline God-silencing medication as well. Like non-religious people who still believe in angels, non-visionary people still accept visions. In that primitive reptilian part of the brain that fears the dark there seems to be an automatic acceptance of mystical events.

Debate rages, however, in all religions and forms of belief about what is the very best (or sometimes the only) way of communication with the Gods. Examining how we communicate with the Gods, there is an easy and obvious division between 'believing' and 'doing'. Traditional Christian theology makes this distinction as between 'faith' and 'works'. On the one hand, all religion necessarily begins with belief; the judgement of an action without belief is merely a moral or a legal system. On the other hand, there is a definite fundamentalist Christian dogma that one's 'works' (that is, one's actions) are always flawed and insufficient and that people are saved (that is granted eternal life in Christianity) through the grace of God. This justification unfortunately can result in the hasty deathbed conversions of lukewarm believers, the refusal of malefactors to accept the consequences of their illegal or immoral actions once they have asked for God's grace, and the selling of sin-forgiving indulgences by the designated Gods-Speakers. On the gripping hand, I feel that whole-hearted belief will necessarily result in good actions because in my theology our communication with the Gods results in Their communication with us which directs action by us as per Their dictates. On our side of the equation we benefit from communication with the Good Gods since a part of Their aim seems to be encouraging us to be our best selves. On Their side of the equation we wonder if the Gods need our actions; is there some benefit to the Gods in our worship and ritual resulting in a channel of communication?

Does our belief benefit the Gods; do the Gods need our actions? Some theologies posit that the number of believers, or sacrifices, or temples add to the power of the specified God. Conversely, some believe that the forgetting of a God (a pre-literate Deity not discovered by archeologists, for instance) causes that God to dwindle. Some post-moderns theorize that the accumulation of belief in the minds of followers 'creates' a specific God-Form from some inchoate Pre-Goddishness. While I am not so simplistic or 'primitive' to believe in a simple power-of-belief equation that amount of bloodshed equals degree of correctness and strength of ritual, I am archaic enough to believe that we are not powerful enough to actually harm the Gods. We can surely harm each other, the fabric of the world around us, and the non-human animals we cultivate or impinge on and undoubtedly this is noticed and felt by Earth Herself and by the Gods who communicate through and on the earth. Are the Gods then powerless to enforce good action and correct belief? No, but another of the universal ideals of humanity is in our free will. In Pagan systems generally wrong action or weak belief results in bad outcome — the land ruled by the selfish king has famine but Bres is not forcibly kept from rude behavior by the Gods, They merely favor the other side. In Christian dogma, one must freely choose correct belief — in a vampire-like pavane Christ must be invited in order to enter and otherwise must linger outside. So universally it would seem that God or the Gods cannot or will not forcibly act on people. They can assist or withhold, heal or blast, send rain and hunting quarry or drought and hunger, but not make puppets out of their believers. Actually, in my theology as an Animist all beings— people, animals, Spirits of Animals, trees, rivers, rocks, Spirits of Place et al can choose to answer a God's expressed wish or decline. In a kind of theistic judo throw, the God is not diminished by our refusal but incorporates it into outcome.

Does our belief in the Gods benefit ourselves, do we need the Gods? Many different 'yes' answers exist. On many scales and in many tests, believers have been found to have happier, healthier, more fulfilling lives than unbelievers. Diseased believers have higher recovery rates than disbelievers, believers rate their personal happiness in higher percentages on polls than disbelievers, believers average longer lives than disbelievers. If the various polls and studies are accurate, belief has tangible this-world benefits. It is impossible, however, to disentangle the societal benefits of social connectedness and peer support for healthy lifestyle from the more arcane benefits than may result in ongoing communication with a God or Gods.

And, still, what is the 'best' means of God-Speaking, the most effective, garnering the most results? All religions and all individual visionaries of course favor their method, the one that works best for them. Trying to evaluate the different modes is a twofold problem. What constitutes success, clarity and amount of communication or degree of beneficial change effected in the measurable world? This then becomes part of the previous 'faith or works' debate. Phrased in a more general, less specifically Christian, way — is orthodoxy (perfect correctness of belief) more or less potent than orthopraxy (perfect correctness of performance)? Opinions vary. Some place great emphasis on the conversional moment — the asking in of Jesus that is pivotal in numerous Fundamentalist Christian religions is one such. Some are vehement for careful and exact dogma — the Catholic Inquisition (also known as the Spanish Inquisition [which no one expects] because Spain so excelled at the exercise) is an historical example but modern examples of religions that require careful and exact interpretation of their Bible abound. Some require perfect implementation of ritual—the Blessing Ways of the Navaho which aim for a combination of perfect sand paintings, perfect chanting and music, and perfect responses by the recipient to be wholly effective. Some religions preach that rescuing perceived blasphemers ('lost sheep') is more important than singing in the choir and some add the idea that numbers of souls saved (that is, whole indigenous populations culturally changed by missionaries) is vital. I see a slight bias towards orthopraxis (doing) in Pagan and Non-Abrahamic religions and orthodoxy (believing) in the Abrahamic ones. Although there is, of course, significant overlap—the Jewish practice of keeping kosher is very action-based and achieving perfect will facilitates success in Ceremonial Magick.

As I said before, all religions and visionaries favor their own method. I endorse trance, mystic vision, and ongoing dedication to specific Gods because those are my methods. The Gods are unable to be polled on Their favorites (perhaps debate rages in Gods-Land as well) so we must work from perceived effects in this world. What effects will we allow as being 'from God'? Again, we are hampered by not being able to ask this question in Gods-Land. There is one way of accessing success, the formation and longevity of a religion created from the received message of a Gods-Speaker. The Mormons (Church of the Latter-Day Saints) is one such, the Heaven's-Gate Cult (the believers who suicided in order to get on board the starship they associated with the Hale-Bopp comet) is a less (by this measure) successful one. There is the measurement of change affected by the actions of the followers or listeners of a specific message; in David Brin's astonishing novel *Earth*, he posits a Church of Gaia which supports the Trillion Trees replanting project. Like real-world religions that measure number of Bibles distributed or amount of donations sent (things that don't effect a change in the earth by their existence) this would be, if actualized, an outcome that created a change by its existence; like building an enormous but also a living Temple.

There is a third kind of appraisal of success, that of a necessary action being performed without which the outcome would change. As a definition, this sounds obscure, but concrete and clear examples abound. The first one that comes to my mind is the Rain Dance (actually the Snake and Antelope Dance to them) performed annually by the Hopi. When it is determined that the correct time has come, a complex and lengthy ritual including personal and community observances is worked through culminating in the Dance in which various important kiva members personify Spirits and ask the Gods to send rain. The implication is that without the ritual and dance there would not be rain, but also that the performance of the entire ritual is an act of communication and sacrifice to the Gods that furthers both the society and the earth. Another example is the persistent story that all of the existing Druid societies banded together during World War II, created an 'Umbrella of Power', and warded off (some) of the enemy bombers coming across the English Channel. A more historical example is that of the long-continuing Mid-Summer offering of a bundle of rushes by the Manx to Mannan beg mac y Leir (the Manx name of the God more commonly known as Manannán mac Lir) as rent for the island which is His home-place. Even the tiny island my Irish ancestors lived on, Iniskea, has a tradition of ritual offering and propitiation. For an unknown length of time, the island had a stone called the Naomhóg on which a poorly documented group of rituals centered. It was ritually dressed in a new suit of clothes at regular intervals and may have had a designated niche it lived in or may have been rotated amongst the island houses. It might have been stolen by the South Islanders from the North Island to enhance the production of potatoes, but all the tales reference its ability to manage sea-storms. All of the other embellishments aside, the Naomhóg kept the fishermen safe. In the end a Catholic priest broke it and tipped it in the South harbor (since he had earlier thrown it whole into the bay only to have it fished back out when he departed for the mainland). He died shortly after, but the island later suffered devastating losses of their young fishermen from a sudden night-storm and moved to the mainland with the heart taken out of them.

What do these examples show us? All of them (and there are many others) demonstrate not only the open communication between the Gods and the participants but also the expectation that the ritual and offering is necessary for ongoing well-being. Without the bundle of rushes, the flannel suit of clothes, the dance, what would happen? Not only the absence of the human-desired outcome— good fishing, safe sailing, and rain for crops— but also natural disasters that affect more than just the participants of the ritual— drought, storms, lack of fish. So, in the context of the participants, they are performing and offering not only for themselves but also for the benefit of all the people who would be affected by their non-performance. From their point of view they are entering into communication with and offering to the Gods of Place who without the human actions will cease to listen and will withdraw Their goodwill.

Does ritual facilitate the continuance of the earth? Do the Gods need us? A qualified yes from me. Ritual, the ceremonious opening and strengthening of the communication between Gods and God-Speakers, allows the people to know what the Gods think and want, what Their instructions are, and the Gods to hear a clearly stated and audible-to-Them assertion of need from the people. What would happen without this? Something else. The Gods would carry on with Their plan without any communication to or from people and the people would only have whatever hindsight their science allows them to plan their future actions with. So Earth wouldn't end; Hertha has weathered larger storms than the actions of people on Her. And the Gods wouldn't end either; They don't need us for Their existence but only as company. And as Their eyelash mites or gut bacteria.

Part 4

Why Now? Modern Day

In a number of religions, these days have been identified as the End Times of the world. World-ending prophecies are common; Ragnarök, the Rapture, the prophecy of Badb at the end of the *Second Battle of Mag Tuired*, the beginning of the Fifth World foretold by the Hopis, and of course the ending of the Mayan calendar. All of these religious predictions have a common thread of the present world catastrophically ending or at least dramatically changing and ushering in a never-ending realm or another quite different cycle of existence. Science has now added its own voice to these auguries, and many post-modern irreligious scientifically exclusive people also identify now as the end time. The biggest difference between 'primitive' world-ending theology and present-day disaster scenarios is the multiplicity and aimlessness of modern dooms. Previously, all members of a religion or society agreed about what was to happen and believed that something (most likely decreed by the Gods) would replace the now-world. Now, each end-world believer has hir own scenario, argues it against all others, and bitterly discredits the competing events believed in by others. Peak Oil! Nuclear Winter! Death of the Oceans! Hole in the Ozone! Climate Change! Hybrid Crop Failure! World-Wide Plagues! As well, many modern doom-sayers also feel that Earth Herself will not make it through the ending.

Why are we in this Hand-Basket and where are we going? Some arguments have been made that simple nomadic hunter-gatherers made large changes on the regions they moved into and other arguments have also pointed out epoch-ending events took place before humans existed; but without a doubt European-based, technological, first-world civilization has an unprecedented effect on the whole fabric of the world. Not just the wide-scale industrialization of everywhere, but also that the technologies of travel, shipping, and communication link us together in a way that has never been experienced before. There is a possibility that global connectedness could enhance the perception that we are all similar, fragile, and valuable (the concept of 'humankind') and encourage tolerance but this does not appear to be the case. Instead there seems to be a terrible lowest-common-denominator applied that everyone wants a car, a cell phone, and a color TV and no one wants a farm. Previously non-industrialized countries jump from walking-pace to cell phones and from cottage manufacturing to importing poisonous first-world garbage in order to kick-start destroying their own ecologies.

'Science' and 'Technology' are being used as a replacement for traditional religion and are being proposed as forming the solution to our current world problems. This even in the face of the fact that Science is nothing more than the 'therefore' clause in a syllogism and Technology is as random as natural selection— many discoveries are nothing more than accidental applications. Science is a way of examining outcome based on replicable results and so replaces religion only in causality, not in intent. Technology, more insidious, creates an ever-faster, ever-smaller loop (as in the cascade telegraph/telephone/tiny hand-held device or movies in theaters/movies on televisions/movies on your tiny hand-held device) that creates enormous hungry markets for products and concurrently enormous piles of poisonous garbage. But in the end both new objects and scientific explanations fall short of perfectly satisfying an age-old (primate-old?) need, the need for belief. As traditional religions lose ground (and generally angrily blame external causes for their falling-off) there is a world-wide surge in newly communicated, newly interpreted religions and also in Neo-Paganism. By 'new' religions I mean those which are purported to be a recent communication to a God-Speaker or an up-dated interpretation of traditional dogma. Neo-Paganism is a regenerated construction referencing some one or several Pre-Abrahamic religions. That is, if one is a traditional Hindu, culturally unchanged First Person in the Americas, or continuing practitioner of Icelandic Asatru you might or might not self-identify as Pagan but you would not be 'Neo'. If you and some like-minded friends read the Eddas, surfed the Internet, and started practicing a Norse religion amongst yourselves you would be 'Neo-Pagans'.

What supports new God-Speaking preachers and followers of revived Old Religions? Partly, I think, just an innate human need for community unsatisfied in this age of large cities, fast movement, and tenuous relationships. As well, many traditional religions are now perceived as tainted by history— in their past they have committed acts, supported biases, or excluded members that in the new age of personal equality are perceived as wrong-headed. A powerful example of this is the tendency of many classic religious dogmas to designate women as lesser than men in function and capability and so to exclude all those people who see humans as inherently equal or at least not limited by their gender as to competence. This 'new age of personal equality' also supports personal as opposed to doctrinal belief. 'I feel it to be so' replaces 'my priest says' and even new God-Speakers generally need to create 'what the leader says resonates in me' rather than unquestioning acceptance.

Globalization (as well as making us all want tiny multi-function hand-held devices) causes a powerful strength of religion, the action of an entire community together towards the end-point of communication with God or Gods, to weaken and dissolve. Confusion and disagreement reign. For example, I took catechetical classes for a while as an adult. The priest and I had a great time and fine discussions because we were both interested in medieval history but we also followed and examined the general instruction book of dogma. At one point he explained that at the point in the Mass when the priest lifts the host to the sound of a bell, "Christ is present". As medievalists, we both found this profoundly satisfying. In later consideration I think that it exemplifies the ineffable moment of immediate communication with the God that all religions and God-Speakers desire. But that moment is not perceived as universally meaningful; when years later I was in conversation with a Lutheran minister and related that story he said witheringly, "And at other times Christ is absent!?!". Or, to tell the story of another example of non-universality, I was for a time a member of a Bible study group. We read the gospel of John together and I was specifically invited as a Pagan because I could be counted on to have "interesting and different opinions". To protect me from proselytization and their group from suspicion of apostasy the members worked out a code; if a visiting minister came the host or hostess would say as I entered the room, "A special treat tonight, Judith! Minister So-and-So of Such-and-Such Church has joined us!" and I was able to decide what I wanted to say or leave unsaid. Once a visiting minister was preaching a truly horrible interpretation of 'many mansions' to universal but tolerant dissatisfaction and two of the members finally stepped up to disagree.

"In our little church Pastor Somebody places a less literal interpretation on that ..."

As it turned out, their little church was a Fundamentalist sect very similar to Visiting Minister So-and-So's except that their church forbade women to wear all jewelry except plain wedding bands and his sect forbade women to wear all jewelry including wedding bands. He turned to them, paused a minute to be sure of the identification, and replied with unimaginable scorn, "Yes, but he and his followers are those RING-WEARING Christians!!"

If, as I think is the case, people believing in unison and acting a ritual of belief in unison is a great facilitator in opening the lines of communication with the Gods then all this squabbling and dissension makes God-Speaking by the congregation far more difficult and diffuse. As well, the loss of a secure place in society and acceptance of their otherness for trained and gifted God-Speakers further muddies the flow. What were once clear-cut religious holy days bringing a community into concerted action have become societal holidays that are universal only in one either having the day off or getting a premium wage to work. For example, when I worked at an animal hospital I always volunteered to work Christmas (societally shortened from Christ's Mass) Day and got Hallowe'en (societally shortened from Hallowed Evening) off instead. I would explain to co-workers that advised me I could force shorter-term employees to work Christmas that I celebrate other holidays than that one and was fine with repeatedly working the day. Without exception, their concern was that by eschewing celebrating Christmas I was missing out. They asked me "But do you get presents!?!" and when I responded that we have a familial present-giving day on First November they were reassured and happy that both they and I benefited from the season. Actually, we have a modern interpretation of the Scandinavian Yule-Cat tradition on that day when we all ceremoniously give each other socks although I generally omitted that information since socks are not what most people want as presents. But the getting of presents, the eating of hollow shaped chocolates, or the begging for tiny candy bars at strangers' doors is not a ritual cycle that will facilitate the continuance of the world.

So, as the needs of increasing industrialization and the falling-off of traditional religions simultaneously globalizes and weakens the expression of belief the need for belief grows commensurately. On our side that need may be an atavistic hold-over from 'primitive' society or it may be the calling out of our in-place Gods-Speaker brain part to be used. But from the Gods' side of the interaction, it may be a concerted effort by a number of Deities and Spirits of Place led by Earth Herself, Hertha, to effect a necessary communication that has dwindled and lapsed. What we hear may not be the fading echo of what once was that heralds the dying gasp of humankind but instead a new and vigorous effort at sending a message that is time after time thwarted by the paucity and ineptitude of non-traditional God-Speakers. Post Modern First World people all wish to be special and remarkable (Indigo Children come to mind) but they generally want to be innately special rather than special through long study and effort. And most of us do not want to be suspected to be crazy nor do we want to follow the commands of a Deity who may or may not fully explain why Ze wants that thing done. The good and progressive ideation that strives to make us all inherently equal and possessing in the fullest sense the free will to make and implement our decisions causes us to suspect and ignore the strange God Voices that speak in our heads and send us directives that often have poorly understood meaning.

Part 5

What Next? Conclusion

Think of it— the very same wonderful idea that frees us from class and caste and makes us each our own individual sovereign also makes us terrible kings: ruder than Balor, greedier than Midas, more self-indulgent than David. What is to be done? Or, again looking at the communication from the other side, what are the Gods telling us needs to be done? There are two things necessary, belief and action. The Gods put the Gods-Speaker in our brains so that we can sing the world-song to the Earth along with the trees, butterflies, grass, rivers, and mountains. Lay your hands on the Great Mother and send Her your love. Then look around at your place, the country of Where You Are, and find something that needs fixing, healing, or helping. And take action.

The orthodoxy (the necessary dogma) of the equation is simple; believe that Earth is alive, Hertha loves us, and we have a responsibility to Her. The orthopraxis (the required doing) is vast and complex. We can plant a trillion trees; we can walk, bike, or take public transportation; we can grow vegetable gardens; we can make laws about emissions ... there is an endless list. My injunction is not to tell you what to do because I am not your God of Place. You need to discover and listen to your own place, your own Spirit of Locale, and by extension communicate with Earth, the home and mother of all of us together. If you do not want to or are not comfortable listening to the answers (not everyone is good at or embraces the Crazy) you can still speak to your place and to Earth and believe that they are listening. You can seek out a trustworthy God-Bothered person (I recommend the "Advanced Bonewits' Cult Danger Evaluation Frame" and using common sense) if you would like to participate in the conversation. Or just find some other people who like the implementation you favor and start doing, knowing that the efforts you are making are being communicated.

What you must do (or actually what I must try to convince you to do by the directive of the Goddess to Whom I am dedicated) is to speak to Earth with words and deeds and your personal Right Action to improve yourself and lessen the destructive impact of your life which will, by reflection, improve and hearten the Earth. She will listen to your message of love for Her and appreciate the loving actions that follow from that caring. You are the Absolute Ruler of Yourself-Land, be an involved and active one; be a Good King.

Moon Books invites you to begin or deepen your encounter with Paganism, in all its rich, creative, flourishing forms.